No Post-Easter Slump

Gospel Sermons For Sundays
After Pentecost (First Third)
Cycle A

Wayne H. Keller

CSS Publishing Company, Inc., Lima, Ohio

NO POST-EASTER SLUMP

Copyright © 1998 by
CSS Publishing Company, Inc.
Lima, Ohio

All rights reserved. No part of this publication may be reproduced in any manner whatsoever without the prior permission of the publisher, except in the case of brief quotations embodied in critical articles and reviews. Inquiries should be addressed to: Permissions, CSS Publishing Company, Inc., P.O. Box 4503, Lima, Ohio 45802-4503.

Scripture quotations are from the *New Revised Standard Version of the Bible*, copyright 1989 by the Division of Christian Education of the National Council of the Churches of Christ in the USA. Used by permission.

Library of Congress Cataloging-in-Publication Data

Keller, Wayne H., 1930-
    No post-Easter slump : Gospel sermons for Sundays after Pentecost (first third) : Cycle A / Wayne H. Keller.
       p. cm.
    ISBN 0-7880-1253-3 (alk. paper)
    1. Bible. N.T. Gospels—Sermons. 2. Pentecost season—Sermons. 3. Sermons, American. I. Title.
BS2555.4.K43   1998
252'.64—dc21   98-9385
                                                                                  CIP

This book is available in the following formats, listed by ISBN:
    0-7880-1253-3   Book

PRINTED IN U.S.A.

*Dedicated to the
Easter-Pentecost Saints
(that is, Christians) who practice
the belief that All of Life is Holy Ground.*

Table Of Contents

Preface   7

Pentecost   9
   Zapped By The Spirit: No Post-Easter Slump
   John 20:19-23

Holy Trinity   13
   Mission — An Identity Crisis
   Matthew 28:16-20

Corpus Christi   19
   Overcoming Spiritual Anemia
   John 6:51-58

Proper 5   23
Pentecost 3
Ordinary Time 10
   Playing It Cool? Not Jesus!
   Matthew 9:9-13, 18-26

Proper 6   27
Pentecost 4
Ordinary Time 11
   Who Me? You've Got To Be Kidding!
   Matthew 9:35—10:8 (9-23)

Proper 7   31
Pentecost 5
Ordinary Time 12
   Having The Right Kind Of Fear
   Matthew 10:24-39

Proper 8   35
Pentecost 6
Ordinary Time 13
    All Of This, And A Reward, Too?
    Matthew 10:40-42

Proper 9   41
Pentecost 7
Ordinary Time 14
    It's Time!
    Matthew 11:16-19, 25-30

Proper 10   45
Pentecost 8
Ordinary Time 15
    4000 Chickens And 2000 Eggs
    Matthew 13:1-9, 18-23

Proper 11   51
Pentecost 9
Ordinary Time 16
    The Eternal Divorce
    Matthew 13:24-30, 36-43

Lectionary Preaching After Pentecost   57

Preface

Sermon one begins with this statement: "Pentecost — the 'religious holiday' ignored by the mass media. Thank God! Pentecost — the Christian holy day neglected by much of the church. Good grief!"

I have no idea how the church forgot, or never remembered, that without Pentecost, Easter would have died on the vine, literally, on the wood of the Cross.

Because much of the mainline church overlooks the Coming-of-the-Spirit-Event, excesses, reaching almost magical proportions, spring up in strange places with strange faces. Forgetting Pentecost, the birthday of the Church, contributes, substantially, to a powerless, impotent community of faith.

No day in the church year excites and energizes me more than the Spirit-Event depicted in Acts 2 — the rushing wind, the flaming tongues, the strange languages, the bewildered people, the transformed Peter, the empowered faithful. At that first Pentecost, the Presence and Power of the Risen Christ transformed the early disciples from kittens to tigers. That can, that does happen today, yes, even among mainline congregations. Red balloons, banners, and bulletins, along with worshipers clothed in red, decorate the sanctuary. A birthday cake awaits the congregation following the celebration.

Two ideas, besides Scripture, guide my sermon preparation for Pentecost and beyond: 1) Jerome Murphy's "If we leave it to the Spirit, there will be nothing left in the church except Jesus and dancing"; and, 2) my "All of life is Holy Ground, so watch where you're stepping."

No season offers more possibilities than Pentecost to put these beliefs into practice.

Pentecost

Zapped By The Spirit: No Post-Easter Slump

John 20:19-23

Pentecost — the "religious holiday" ignored by the mass media. Thank God! Pentecost — the Christian holy day neglected by much of the church. Good grief! "Did you receive the Holy Spirit when you were baptized?" "Receive it? I've never even heard of it!" That's still true of some church members. Others reflect on Peter's remark following Jesus' death. "Okay, boys. It's all over. No point sticking around here. Let's go home and go fishing." Still others shy away from Pentecost because they have bizarre images about strange languages which embarrass them.

Indeed, on a Sunday morning long ago, the disciples expected no sun to rise. Their dreams and plans had come to a screeching halt. Shattered by Jesus' arrest and death, they dropped out one by one: Judas, Peter, Thomas, all but John and a few women; and even they expected never to see him alive again. They would wrap his body in burial clothes, shed a few confused tears, and return to the same old way of life. Perhaps, occasionally, they would think of that pied piper of Bethlehem who had hypnotized them for a time, but who finally met the fate of all who double-cross the politicians and clergy. For centuries, God had promised the Messiah. Surely, the Messiah should have claimed a better fate than a cross. And besides, as those discombobulated disciples angrily mused, "What had he done for them?" The Romans and the clergy still stood guard over their future. A fine Messiah! And now, he was "crucified, dead, and buried." They would pay their last respects, and go home to their families, friends, and fishing boats.

I

Then, the unexpected happened, not magically as some David Copperfield illusion. The unexpected happened because, for some "strange" reason, they decided not to act on Peter's urging. They stayed in Jerusalem. They dug into the Apostles' teaching; they shared the sacrament; they prayed fervently; they continued celebrating together. That's how they, in Christ's Spirit, began the revolution. And, wonder of wonders, Jesus appeared, stood in their presence, and spoke those life-changing words, "Peace be with you ... Receive the Holy Spirit!" When they saw the risen Christ, when they heard those dynamite words, no longer would they drag along in the same old ruts. No longer would they merely shuffle through their daily routines of getting up, dressing, eating breakfast, going to work, returning home, reading the paper, eating supper, going to bed, getting up ... Christ's healing power and *dunamis* (our word for TNT/dynamite) restored them to wholeness from their "barbed-wire" sickness, that "sickness unto death" described by Soren Kierkegaard; that sickness which hemmed them in, tied them down, isolated them from that Eternal Personality who alone brings purpose to life and life to purpose. When receiving Holy Spirit, the Presence and the Power of the living Christ, they finally internalized the objective events of Good Friday and Easter. They moved out into a world dying to hear the Good News. No Pentecost! No Easter!

II

Thank God for Pentecost, the birthday of the church, when the Holy Spirit transformed the disciples from kittens to tigers, setting them on fire, as people convicted, converted, consecrated to set about setting the world right side up. They became victors, rather than remaining victims. They became revolutionaries, rather than rejects. The Christ who died for them became the Christ who lived in and with and through them.

III

God makes the same promise to us. "Peace be with you. Receive the Spirit." T. A. Kantonen, in his book, *A Theology of Christian*

Stewardship, says "No one can be a Christian ... until the Holy Spirit has led him and her into the presence of the living Christ, and a genuine personal commitment to Christ has taken place." So, the question for us today, and for every day, is both simple and profound, "Do we really want Holy Spirit convicting, convincing, converting, changing, challenging us?"

One day, a man asked his pastor, "Why can't I receive power, as did the early disciples, and do the same things as Paul, Steven, the disciples, and multitudes of people since?" The pastor responded, "You shall receive power when Holy Spirit has come upon you. How did *they* prepare to receive the Spirit? How do *you*?" That parishioner had the same hesitation as many of us. M. G. Kyle once said that "all of us pray for Holy Spirit; but as soon as the tongues of flame appear, we run for the fire department."

Holy Spirit that takes root in our lives upsets everything. Christ's presence leaves us dissatisfied with the way we are. No longer can we look for scapegoats, refuse to show mercy to others, play the church game.

We receive Holy Spirit no differently from the disciples. They prayed; they participated in worship; they studied the Scriptures; they received the sacraments. And the Spirit began to transform them into new people, not perfect, but new people, with new attitudes, motives, behaviors. They obeyed. One day, a young woman who had frequented taverns, asked her pastor if he knew the dirtiest word used in such places. Reluctantly, he said, "No." Without a moment's hesitation, she said, "Commitment!"

Obedience, discipline, commitment — that is our response to our receiving the Good News. Of course, we would rather have meetings, talk about prayer, avoid forgiving our enemies, expect worship to comfort us, and focus on the nonessentials. Charles Schulz, in his book *Teenager Is No Disease,* has one of the characters ask, "Do you think that anyone is interested in the number of hot dishes the church has served since the Day of Pentecost?" It's possible that we spend more time talking about potlucks after worship than we spend sharing our experience of Christ at any time.

IV

How do we avoid the potluck syndrome? How do we receive Holy Spirit? No differently from the disciples. Too simple? Too scary? Too demanding? Too demeaning for us sophisticated "modern" folks? The disciples put themselves in a position where Holy Spirit could change them. They worshiped. Worship was top priority, not something they did in their spare time when they had nothing better to do. In the Pacific Northwest, church members, on the average, attend worship once a month. The disciples prayed. They put God to the test. They spoke honestly, and sometimes bluntly, knowing that God could handle any complaint or request. They recognized and accepted their oneness in Christ despite their incredible diversity. They knew that "only the disciplined change the world." They discovered, beyond a shadow of a doubt, "that before God sent the church into the world, God sent the Spirit into the church." (John Stott)

The nitty-gritty of Christianity, Paul summarized in these words: "If you want the Spirit, build the church" (1 Corinthians 14:12). "Get in and give it a hand. Criticize it, yes ... in love. Build it up. Stop tearing it down, either by outright antagonism or by deadly apathy."

Someone has said that "evangelism occurs when people are so kindled with the central fire of Christ that they, in turn, set others on fire." So what the church needs, and what we need if we want the Spirit, are people who allow God to overpower them, who admit that they don't have all the answers, who recognize a need for each other, who share both their strengths and weaknesses, who show their humanity and vulnerability. In that spirit, no post-Easter slump for them!

How about us? How will you/we be in the Spirit today, this week? How will we reveal ourselves as the presence and power of the Christ in this world now?

Hallelujah! The Christ is alive! Your life and mine, from this day forward, will never be the same. And now, to remember this Pentecost event, the ushers will hand out to each of you an invitation to the Birthday Party which began long ago, and which comes today and every day.

Holy Trinity

Mission — An Identity Crisis

Matthew 28:16-20

The church, that is, the *ekklesia*, the called out ones, has taken some hard knocks both from its friends within and its foes without, from chilly indifference inside and arrogant cynicism outside. All kinds of people have condemned it for its navel-gazing, and its lack of concern for the world. Some years ago in Russia, two meetings took place simultaneously. In one, a group of Marxists discussed how they could overturn the world. In the other, which took place only a few doors away, a group of Christians fervently debated the color of their church's choir robes. Despite its preoccupation with trivia, the church still stands, perhaps healthier than for many years. For today, the church, despite its near asphyxiation during the 1950s, that part of it possessed by Holy Spirit, takes the world seriously. It's true, the church, some of it, continues to make a fool of itself; but thank God, the church, some of it, has moved from a fool to an asset. Yes, it still stumbles, bumbles, mumbles, tumbles, as it seeks to grasp its purpose in a world changing with every sunrise. T. S. Eliot once described the church as a "fat hippopotamus resting on its belly in the mud." But no longer is it quite so fat in the belly, or so flat in the mud. The church, some of it, has begun to arouse from its slumber, to wake from its sleep, and to shake off its sluggishness. Here, in capsule form, summarizes what has begun to happen: "A realization, an awareness that God has called the *ekklesia* from the world, to the institution, to send it back into the world."

I

In the past, some have lopped off the last part of the formula. Some think that God calls people from the world into the church, period; even as some parents bring a child into their home, but who never permit the child to leave home emotionally. In a family counseling session, the mother of her 32-year-old son and his wife stated bluntly and arrogantly, "What *you* do is *our* business."

When we hole ourselves up in the activities of the church institution, when we pull out of the world, or refuse to enter it in the first place, we are heretics. If we become so preoccupied with the institution by insisting on fancy buildings, to impress the community; bigger and better budgets, to buy spiritual services; popular preachers, to tickle our fancies; a multiplicity of clubs and organizations, to fulfill our social and recreational needs; and a music director, with choirs for every age — if we become so enamored with these, we may never hear, with our heart and will, the Great Commission.

These criteria, too often, have become our guidelines for defining the "successful church." We can easily sacrifice quality for quantity. And when this happens, church rolls balloon, buildings and mortgages skyrocket. Persons who consider themselves fine, respectable, white Americans sign the dotted line, missing the whole point that God expects a change of heart, and will, and purpose, and pocketbook in the lives of God's people. And the commission of Christ to his disciples, then and now, gets lost in the shuffle, gets buried in institutional paraphernalia, busyness, popularity, trivia.

II

Today, with some, the image has changed. The church has begun to move back into the world with Christ's message of reconciliation, with an urgent involvement in the world to which God sent Jesus. We recall that good old First Church of Jerusalem in 66 A.D. died because it had attached itself to Jewish rites, and contented itself by remaining a Jewish sect. No doubt, parish activities were going full tilt; but the church was dead in its relation to God. It discovered, as many churches have since, that a congregation, or an individual Christian, which no longer moves out in the Spirit of Christ, literally passes out in the spirit of death.

When Christ calls us Christians to "go therefore and make disciples of all nations, baptizing them in the name of the Father, and of the Son and of the Holy Spirit," Christ insists that we invade every sphere of life, beginning with the family next door, and extending into the realms of politics, economics, environment, recreation, credit-buying, and overindulging. We Christians have no options, though we like to think that we do. Edwin T. Dalberg, formerly with the National Council of Churches, said a long time ago, "Too many of us have become Fifth-Amendment Christians. We are refusing to be witnesses for our Lord and declining to testify for Christ lest we incriminate ourselves, and become too much involved with the Kingdom of God and the Cross of Calvary."

Unfortunately, some of us have engaged in reversed-evangelism. We have demanded that the church cater to our whims, agree with our ideas; and when that doesn't happen, we quit outright, or become Christmas-Easter members. We give God the leftovers after indulging ourselves in the latest gadgets and newest models. We ignore our opportunities for the good witness. We criticize everything that we don't like; and we think that we have fulfilled our responsibility to Christ and the world. So, when Christ calls us to go back into the world, we refuse to go, when actually, we need to refuel to go.

III

So, how do we go back into the world as a congregation, as individual Christians? First, we need to accept the fact that we already are in all the world, about 167 hours per week. In the world, we have multitudes of opportunities to witness.

A. As a congregation, for example, have we ever dared to tackle a job too big for us? Do we dare, do we even dare to think of attempting a job so great that we might go under as a congregation? Are we willing to set our mission at fifty percent of our total income, and pay it before any local bills, including the pastor's salary? Are we more concerned about the world out there than we are about ourselves in here? Would it hurt us to sit in a cold, unlit sanctuary, even for one Sunday, to remind us of the millions who spend their entire lives in the cold and dark? Would it ruin our security and comfort to let our relatives and neighbors know that the church has top priority in our lives? One pastor's parents informed their relatives that if they came to visit on Sunday morning, they could sit in the driveway, or come to worship with them. Would this congregation survive if, for one year, we had no pastor in order to free that money for world mission? Would we damage our reputation if we closed the church school to our own children, so that children of nonmembers could use the space? Are we willing to dream dreams about what the church might do to be the church in mission?

B. As individual Christians, how much do we care about the world, the immediate community, which has no relation to Christ and the church? Do we care about the lonely, frightened people around us who cover their loneliness and fear with their masks of false superiority and clever dishonesty; or by owning everything that money can buy; or by excelling at everything they do, because they can't stand to fail? Will we, to whom God has given the greatest news of all time, share that news with people with whom we play cards, go on picnics, attend movies, have barbecues, and talk about everything under the sun, except our friendship with Christ?

One congregation uniquely uses the "potluck suppers," not family potlucks in the church building, but suppers in homes. Invitations to the neighbors, some church-related, some not, to come in for supper, and to have a wide-open discussion on religion, or any related topic, has met with a fine response. The church members found that "outsiders" in the neighborhood were waiting for an opportunity to have this kind of fellowship, so different from the superficiality of the cocktail party, or the after-worship coffee hour. Are we willing to "go into the world" in this sense? These neighbors of ours may never know that "God cared enough to send the very best," unless and until we, God's people, first demonstrate by word and deed, that we care enough to be the very best that God sent. Presbyterians, many years ago, coined the phrase, "Friendship Evangelism." Too often, we have emphasized friendship without evangelism.

We learn to care, to show compassion, only as we expose ourselves to each other in some degree of depth. We learn to care, not by standing on the sidelines and throwing rocks, but by sharing ourselves with one another. We learn to care when we know that other Christians care about us, as we are, with no strings attached.

In a cartoon, a doctor refers to his patient as a "gall bladder in 909." That description, of course, dehumanizes his patient. Christ calls us to trust each other as persons, literally, as though we are the other, not that nasty person down the street, but that person who hurts so badly she can relate to no one; not that sour-joe at the office, but that person whose wife just left him; not that alcoholic on skid row, but that person whose life has crashed on the rocks; not that obnoxious spouse of ours, but that person who first must learn how to relate in our quirks.

Christ's mission, and therefore ours, is to these — not to criticize, castigate, clobber, condemn, but to console, comfort, confront, counsel. When we accept Christ's mission as ours, as Christ's mission through us, then, we begin to understand Christ's commission to "go into all the world" for his sake, for the world's sake, and yes, for our sake also.

From the world to the church back into the world. Go into all the world, knowing that our greatest witness is our deepest relationship of love. That is the church in action. That is the church in mission. That's where we are. That's who we are, for Christ's sake, under Christ's direction, in Christ's power.

Corpus Christi

Overcoming Spiritual Anemia

John 6:51-58

Webster, the famous dictionary author, defines *anemia* as a "condition in which the red corpuscles of the blood are reduced in number, or deficient in hemoglobin, causing pallor, shortness of breath, and palpitation of the heart." Because of this condition, an anemic person lacks vigor and vitality. If we care about our health, we know what to do about physical anemia. Without delay, we seek medical advice, and hopefully, a cure.

I

We not so quickly detect spiritual anemia; and even when we do, we are somewhat slower doing anything about it. Life rolls along, as slow as Old Man River. No particular problems dog us. Oh, we may feel a slight tinge of restlessness. We know that something is missing, but we can't quite put our finger on it. We shake it off, "I must be at an awkward age"; or "I need a new job, a vacation, in Hawaii." Or perhaps, "If only I moved to a new neighborhood, or had another child, or got a salary increase, or added another car to the garage, or found a new friend, or changed spouses, my life would take a turn for the better." We hope that once we revise or change our external circumstances, then our life will take on new proportions and dimensions. Then, our life will become robust, healthy, filled with the joy and peace for which we have worked and waited so long. So we complete the outer rituals. We rearrange the furniture. We acquire everything on which we can lay our hands. Still, we feel anxious, weak, frustrated, broken, empty, useless. We have found no cure for our spiritual anemia.

II

We cry out, "Who will prescribe something that will heal us, cure us, make us whole and healthy persons? We tried materialism. It failed. We tried humanism. It failed. We tried technology. It failed. We tried freedom without restraints. It failed. What can make us well?"

Augustine once insisted that "we are restless until we rest in God." Is that the answer? Is God, as revealed in the Christ, the right prescription? Does wholeness come as we reside in the forgiveness, confidence, and trust of God? The church says, "Yes." Such rest comes, not from a good night's sleep, or an afternoon nap. It comes from a knowledge that the God who made us also sustains and nourishes us; from an acceptance of Christ as personal Savior and living Lord; from a confidence that the Spirit refuses to desert us, even though we do our best to hide from the Presence and Power again and again.

III

In no act of the church do we experience healing from spiritual anemia more convincingly than in the Sacrament of the Lord's Supper. Hear these words of John: "... unless you eat the flesh of the Son of Man and drink his blood, you have no life in you ... Those who eat my flesh and drink my blood abide in me, and I in them."

The bread and the cup provide us with the vitamins, calories, minerals to make healthy spirits. The bread and the cup fill us with the courage to face the burdens of life, with the tenderness of sacrificial service, with the assurance of a victorious future. And all of this is possible because Jesus cared enough to give himself to stir our spirits, to save us from ourselves and our false gods, and to bring us to our ultimate victory in God's power.

The Christ now invites us to share with him in the ministry of sacrificial love. William L. Stidger tells the story of a man in his congregation who joined the Navy during World War II. One night, during a Boston layover, the Naval officer stopped to visit his pastor. Now the captain of a large transport, he told Dr. Stidger how he had guided his ship in a convoy across the Atlantic during a submarine attack. In one fatal moment, he noticed the white mark of a torpedo headed directly toward his ship loaded with hundreds of soldiers. He had no time to change course. Through the loudspeaker, he shouted, "Boys, this is it!" Nearby appeared a destroyer, whose captain had also seen the torpedo. With no hesitation, he shouted, "Full speed ahead!" The destroyer swiftly maneuvered into the path of the torpedo, and took its full impact. It sank with all the crew. After telling the story, the transport captain remained silent. Then, looking at his pastor, he said, "Dr. Stidger, the skipper of that destroyer was my best friend." Again, he remained silent for some time. Then, slowly he said, "You know, there is a verse in the Bible which has special meaning to me now. It is this: 'Greater love has no one than this, that we lay down our life for our friends.' " (Source of illustration lost.)

To paraphrase what Jesus says, "As the living Father sent me, and I live because of the Father, so those who eat of my body and drink of my blood will live because of me."

The cure for spiritual anemia comes from receiving the bread and wine into our life, and from losing oneself in a cause greater than ourself, a cause which reaches out to shaking limbs, tottering lives, and anxious hearts of fearful, lonely, discouraged persons; to a world ricocheting between life and death. We will not, we cannot heal ourselves. The living Christ can, will cure our anemic life by his love, with his church, through his sacrament.

Proper 5 • *Pentecost 3* • *Ordinary Time 10*

Playing It Cool? Not Jesus!

Matthew 9:9-13, 18-26

"Good grief, Jesus, do you know what you're saying and doing? How often are you going to irritate people before you finally learn your lesson? It seems to us disciples that you're deliberately setting yourself up for another 'kick me' game. When will you ever learn the difference between deliberate antagonism and healthy confrontation? Surely, you're aware that you're flirting with disaster when you continue to rail, *ad nauseam*, against the scribes and Pharisees? Keep talking this way, and your days are numbered. So, watch it! Back off before you commit political and religious suicide."

I

The Scripture speaks plainly that Jesus, seeing Matthew sitting at the IRS office, said simply, "Follow me." And Matthew did. Who knows why? Maybe he identified with those who called Jesus "enemy"; for he, too, was enemy to many because of his vocation, often accompanied by graft and extortion. Or, perhaps Jesus had noticed Matthew hanging around on the fringes of the crowd, listening with growing interest to what the Master Teacher had to say about a God willing to forgive our sin, giving us a new chance in life; or about a God who insists that we will find greater joy in giving than in getting. Then again, perhaps Matthew had spoken with Jesus more than once; and Jesus knew that the tax collector was dissatisfied with the kind of life he was living, and that, now, the time had come for him to make a decision. Jesus surely saw the potential in Matthew and zeroed in on that potential.

One day, a long time ago, a sixteen-year-old boy was baptized and joined the church, not because he wanted to, but because his parents expected him to do so. Prior to that Sunday, he and his father hunted or fished almost every weekend. He had no joy sharing the new-found faith of his parents. In worship, Mother sat on one side of him, Father on the other, as he fumed. He did participate in the church's life, all of it, because he had no choice. At age eighteen, he still had no zeal to give up his atheism. One day, however, the pastor shocked him into a new thought. "Have you ever considered entering the seminary and the pastoral ministry?" The young man chuckled, sarcastically, to himself. "How could a nonbeliever become a pastor?" Nevertheless, for the next two years, that question haunted him. And then, after some life-changing experiences, he became a Christian, entered the seminary, and ultimately, the pastoral ministry.

The teenager's pastor saw something in his young parishioner that, in no way, could he, himself, begin to imagine. "How could a shy, fearful, didn't-know-what-to-say-when-someone-said-hello person possibly minister to others?" For forty years in the pastoral ministry, he did minister in exciting, energizing, and productive ways to all kinds of people.

Jesus saw in Matthew what no one else saw. Most had contempt for him and his tawdry profession. Jesus looked beyond the external appearances into Matthew's heart to discover a life waiting to blossom and flower. And so did that pastor looking at that frightened teenager.

We have a multitude of opportunities to speak the good news, not in some forced way, not through some evangelism program, not by some contrived denominational method. We play cards, go on picnics, attend ball games, visit across the backyard fence every day of our lives. And, in those relationships, people reveal themselves, their pain, their anxiety, their questions, their frustrations, as well as their joys, to us every day of their lives and ours. We needn't bludgeon them over the head, or embarrass them into silence, or ridicule them into the Kingdom. We do need to listen, not only, or even primarily, to their words, but to their feelings beneath the words; reflect those feelings, and then offer the invitation to experience new life. A filmstrip, produced by the Presbyterian Church years ago, has one of the characters say, "Your greatest witness is your deepest relationship of love." We change no one. We leave that to Christ's Spirit. We simply offer, and offer simply, ourselves as "good-news sharers."

II

Today's text begins with Jesus' invitation to Matthew, "Follow me." That invitation opened the door to a multitude; for "many tax collectors and sinners came and sat down with Jesus and the disciples." Jesus knew exactly what he was doing, and the results of his actions. And the clergy never missed an opportunity to jab him with their sarcastic barbs. "Why does your teacher," they complained to the disciples, rather than directly to Jesus, "why does your teacher eat with tax collectors and sinners?" "How dare he fraternize with those who weren't the religious elite; those who were trapped, strapped, zapped in their old ways of life; those who were rejected, ostracized, segregated, shut off from all social contacts with the respected, the hoi polloi of society?"

Selective membership still haunts today's church. We want our kind in our church. Some suggest that keeping the church similar to ourselves is the only way to grow a congregation. We need different kinds of churches for people of different races, cultures, genders. We want fellow church members with whom we can feel comfortable, not ill-at-ease. One pastor spent months visiting, inviting some chicken farmers to worship. Finally, after dozens of invitations, they came. Dressed in their chicken-house overalls, they carried the aroma of manure into the sanctuary. They sat in the back row. No one spoke to them. Guess what? They never returned. We prefer to keep ourselves unsullied from the world, surrounded by our kind. We have made the church comfortable, respectable. And some go elsewhere if anyone invades their comfort zone.

If that's our agenda, we will hear from Jesus what the Pharisees heard. "Those who are well have no need of a physician, but those who are sick. Go and learn what this means, 'I desire mercy, not sacrifice.' For I have come to call not the righteous but sinners."

Jesus can minister only to those who recognize their need. He has no way of changing those who think that they have all of the answers, not only for themselves, but for everyone else. The most dangerous church members are those who require that everyone conform to their brand of Christianity, as they carefully select the Scriptures which "prove their point," and ignore those which contradict them and their beliefs. Be aware of the "biblical" debates in regard to abortion and homosexuality. For the extremists boldly claim what no Christian dare claim. "Kill the abortionists and homosexuals." This attitude led to the Inquisition and the Crusades. "Death to all who oppose God's will; I alone know God's will; I alone am righteous. Therefore, I am God's instrument of judgment."

Such an attitude infests and infects both persons and congregations. A 25-year-old church in Washington State had five permanent pastors. All of them left the church in crisis, and all of them left the pastoral ministry. Yet the leadership of the church continues to boast, "We have no problems here." The power structure even today continues to blame the pastors for all of the problems. Denial is a "wonderful" tool for effecting no change. In no way can the Spirit of Christ heal the "super righteous." However, the Scripture promises that those who refuse to "face the music" on their death day, will ask, "When did we see you hungry, thirsty, in prison, sick ... and not minister to you?"

Jesus' message is clear and direct, whether we hear it and respond to it or not. Either we learn to live with each other, beginning in our own homes and congregations, or we will die with each other. For God, in Christ, has called the *ekklesia*, the called out ones, to risk popularity, prestige, power to be and to do the mission. We can sit and moan in the makings of our own Egyptian slavery; or we can move out into the wilderness wanderings, having no idea what will happen next. We can be assured that, whatever happens, Christ has gone before, and Christ empowers us along our journey, no matter what the pain. For in Christ's presence, power, perseverance, we also experience his joy, his love, his victory! Amen!

Proper 6 • *Pentecost 4* • *Ordinary Time 11*

Who Me? You've Got To Be Kidding!

Matthew 9:35—10:8 (9-23)

Unlike many businesses today engaged in the process of "downsizing," it was time for Jesus to "upsize." Too much happening, too many demands, too many needs, too much illness, too many people sapping Jesus' strength. So, he called the twelve. Did he have any idea what he was doing? What a pathetic band of characters, at least by society's standards. In a choose-up-sides baseball game, the captain probably would have picked them last. They looked and acted like the "Charlie Browns" of the first century. Yet, he must have seen something in them, despite their quirks, that they could not see in themselves.

Without Jesus' initiative, the disciples perhaps would have had a lifetime experience similar to Mary-Alice in Patricia Ryan's *George and Other Parables*. "Mary-Alice had potential. It was the first thing anyone noticed when they met her ... After a while, Mary-Alice became frightened. 'What if I should lose my potential ...' So ... Mary-Alice kept her potential stuffed under the mattress. She soon discovered that the lump under the mattress made it difficult to sleep. Mary-Alice packed up her potential and took it to a bank on the far side of town. She rented a large safe-deposit box and locked her potential away in the vault. Faithfully, on the third Tuesday of every month, Mary-Alice would visit her potential. Cautiously, she would peek into the box ... Then she would lock it up again and store her potential safely back in the vault. Feeling quite content, Mary-Alice would take the bus home ... secure in the knowledge that if nothing else, she would always have potential."[1]

Thank God, somehow, in some way, God sends us persons who see in us what we do not see in ourselves. Jesus had that uncanny ability to see a person's potential, and so do many of Jesus' followers.

I

All of the biblical characters spent considerable effort and energy denying their potential, and thus, their use to God, God's church, God's world. Listen to a few. Moses complained, "Who me? I can't do it; I'm no public speaker; I've never been to Toastmasters." Abraham groaned, "Who me? I can't do it; I'm too old." Jeremiah whined, "Who me? I can't do it; I'm only a kid." Jonah grumbled, "I can't do it; I just don't wanna." Peter moaned, "Who me? I can't do it; I'm no Ph.D." Paul grieved, "Who me? I can do it; I'm a murderer!" And the list goes on, *ad infinitim, ad nauseam*, right into the present moment. We, too, raise the "who me?" question, and plead, "I can't do it; find someone else." Our rationalizations and justifications remind us of a *Saturday Evening Post* cartoon, in which one primitive man, observing a pagan religious ceremony, says to his friend, "It's impressive, but I find dial-a-prayer more convenient." With some of us, our faith commitment reflects that spoken by Earl Loomis. "We refuse to recognize our assets; because once recognizing them, we are required to use them." God calls and we rebel, "I won't, and you can't make me!"

II

Yet, God refuses to drop us like a hot potato. Psalm 23:6, in the Hebrew language, promises, "Of a certainty! My covenant grace and my steadfast love shall *hotly pursue* you all the days of your lives...." God, having created us in God's image, tracks us down, as a bloodhound tracks down a wanted criminal. God pursues! The Old Testament characters, despite digging in their heels, finally offer a reluctant "yes," and bring a new dimension to the world of their day. The disciples, sometimes screaming and scratching and struggling, offer a hesitant "yes," and change the world for all time. God still pursues! And how do we respond?

A Presbyterian pastor one day said to his mother, "I hate God about fifty percent of the time. God disturbs me, forces me to change, to select priorities, to remain disturbed with the status quo." He reflected Martin Luther's words, "I hate God"; and that of the preschool child, "I don't like Jesus; he makes me brush my teeth every night." Such honesty will never defeat God.

We need to recall that God's Spirit startles us, rocks us at the core of our life, for God sees something in us that we do not see, maybe, do not want to see, in ourself. When we recognize our potential, and receive God's Spirit, God sends us out into a frightened, confused, anxious world — and not alone. God promises us, provides us with Holy Spirit, the power, God's power, which enlivens, enthuses, energizes us. God transforms us from kittens to tigers, from minnows to whales. God takes us where we are, with our insecurity, our fears, our cowardice, and sends us into a new direction, with a new heart, mind, will. One of the early church fathers insists that the "glory of God is man/woman fully alive!" That's the kind of person God remakes when we get beyond the "Who me? You've got to be kidding!"

Our stewardship of life, resulting from a thanksgiving/thanksliving response, becomes a reflex action of the gift of agapé, the gift of Holy Spirit. We breathe in God's presence; we breathe out God's power. Have we ever wondered if Barabbas, the one whose place Jesus took, ever asked the question to himself, if to no one else, "How will I now live my life?" Do we ever ask that question because of what God in Christ has done, is doing, and will continue to do for, in, with and through us? How does the giving of ourself respond to God's gift of Self?

III

How well do we listen to God's call? How well do we act on what we hear? To share what's going on *with* us, we need to know what's happening *in* us. Continually, we need to take a good look at ourself, and take responsibility for what we see. In God's Kingdom, we no longer need to search for scapegoats. As God's person, we risk ourselves, despite our fears; because we believe that in our every contact with one another, we encourage him/her to live or die. Let me say that again: As God's person, we risk ourselves, despite our fears; because we believe that in our every contact with one another, we encourage him/her to live or die. Let's think about that for a moment. In God's power, we can stop discounting our power. The power reminds us that "no act of kindness ever goes unheeded."

A church member found herself waited on by a grumpy saleslady. Judith decided to put her faith into practice. She knew that how she related to that lady, in those few moments, could and would influence the day for both of them. So, she made eye contact, smiled, spoke pleasantly. And, at least for a few minutes, the saleslady's demeanor changed. God has given us similar gifts. We choose how we relate to one another, no matter how the other relates to us. Thank God for Jesus who chose to relate in caring ways, even as they slapped him in the face, slapped him on the Cross, slapped him in the ground, and slapped him into the tomb.

One church member looks at us church people as manure. If we fail to spread the manure, it sits in a pile. Either it gets dry and brittle and breaks apart; or, it gets wet and soggy and rots. Neither response suits Christians. In response to God's act on our behalf, we are called to live in and to share Christ's love with the world around us, beginning in our own home and congregation. We do this by example. Not enough. We do this with words. Not enough. As Christ's people, we put them together.

So, do we believe that God calls, energizes, sustains us? Do we know that we have received "The Gift Incomparable"? If we do, we share it. If we don't, we won't. That choice, we make every day of our lives, both verbally and non-verbally, consciously and unconsciously. In obedience to the living Christ, who matches our potential with his power, lives the reality of a revolution. You are invited to participate, in the Name of God, the Creator, Liberator, Sustainer, Energizer.

---

1. Patricia Ryan, *George and Other Parables* (Allen, Texas: Argus Communication, 1972). Used by permission of Pricilla Wyman.

Proper 7 • *Pentecost 5* • *Ordinary Time 12*

Having The Right Kind Of Fear

Matthew 10:24-39

Lucy, the psychiatrist of *Peanuts* fame, sits waiting in her booth. Frieda comes seeking help. "My problem is that I'm afraid of kindergarten. I don't even know why! I try to reason it out, but I can't ... I'm just afraid ... I think about it all the time ... I'm really afraid...." Lucy responds, as only Lucy does, "You're no different from anyone else. Five cents, please." Sensitivity never was her primary quality.

I

Nevertheless, Lucy nailed the issue. Frieda is you and I. We all have fears, some real, some imaginary, yet real to us; some healthy, some unhealthy; some known to us, others unknown to us. But have them, we do!

How do we identify or describe them? We look at several possibilities. We may fear that others don't like us, and certainly wouldn't like us if they knew our inner thoughts and outer behaviors. So we do what multitudes do. Instead of risking ourselves, including those with whom we live, we keep everything bottled up inside, thus avoiding true intimacy. Or, we fear that we will not measure up to standards of success or conduct which others set for us. A patient in a mental hospital expressed his guilt and anxiety, because he failed to do what others, beginning with his parents, expected of him. Others of us fear what might happen to our mate and children if anything ever happened to us. Often, those who express such fears fail to make preparations for their own illness and death. We may also fear the loneliness and isolation of growing old and becoming worn out, unable to care for ourself. On the geriatric unit of a hospital, several patients spoke of their lack of energy and purpose, wondering what tomorrow would bring, which for many would be no different from what today brought. We probably agree with what Frederick Speakman says in his book, *Love is Something You Do*. "Do you realize how much of the time we spend running scared among silly amusements and slippery morals to keep from facing how frightened we are?"

So, as frightened animals cowering in the corner, we may spend a lifetime of fear hiding behind our criticism of others who refuse to live up to our standards. Or, we may hole up in our comfortable little communities by revolving our life around our immediate family. Or, in our social groups, we talk about everything under the sun, except who's hurting, who's in pain. Instead, we prefer to keep playing our emotional games, described in Petula Clark's song, "Games People Play." Or, we identify with our church clique in which we all think the same thoughts and complain about the same political and religious issues. Or, we prefer to think of our nation as virtuous, while condemning other nations for not accepting our values and agenda.

If we persist in harboring our illusions, we may well find ourselves responding to life and death as the man in the story, "The Croquet Player." "What if the world does end tomorrow, since there's nothing I can do about it. I don't even want to think about it. I've a date to play croquet with my aunt at 2:00 p.m.; for croquet is at least one thing I can understand." This attitude, this decision, of course, makes us no less frightened. It simply shoves our phobia into our subconscious, where, one day, it may become a neurosis or psychosis.

II

So, is there a brave way to be scared? Ashley Montague, in his book *On Being Human*, says, "Yes," because "to be human is to be in danger." No one ought to be more willing to take risks for the right reasons than the person of faith. Jesus offers a powerful response to our usual fears. "Do not fear those who kill the body but cannot kill the soul; rather fear him who can destroy both body and soul in hell." The early church took that literally, as "the blood of the martyrs became the seed of the church." Despite their fears about getting tossed to the lions, nailed to crosses, sawn in half, they stood and died in the power of the risen Christ. They acted upon the potent belief that the final judgment of life's issues is made, not before human courts, based on personal opinions, even on those made by political and religious gurus, but before the court of God. "Fear not!" Jesus' words echo down the corridor of time. Fear not, for our lives consist, not in the abundance of our plentiful possessions, or personal opinions, or political decisions, but by every word that proceeds from God's mouth.

III

In the power of Christ, we can discard our false fears of power, pride, prejudice, planning, yes, even peacemaking. We do so because we know that we are of infinite worth in God's sight. A Christmas card for the pastor read, "To a member of the NAORBP — National Association Of Really Beautiful People." Fear not! God has more concern for us, the highest creation, than for the hairs on our head (thank God) and for the birds of the air.

Perhaps more than anything we need to learn how to distinguish between essential and nonessential fear. Remember the story of the Gadarene madman in Scripture? When the crowds saw the former madman "sitting clothed and in his right mind," they were afraid. Strange — more afraid of sanity than madness. Maybe we all are. At any rate, it's a fact that while our forefathers and mothers looked forward to automation, we are almost threatened to death by it. Someone has begun a group called "The Lead Pencil Society," as a protest against the mechanical devices of our age.

Soren Kierkegaard, in his book *Purity of Heart Is to Will One Thing*, puts fear in its proper perspective. "Spiritually understood, there is a ruinous illness, (namely) not to fear what a man (woman) should fear, sacredness of modesty, God in the heavens, commands of duty, voice of conscience, accountability to eternity."

Life and reality lie in the realm of knowing what to fear, and what not to fear. Again, the Scripture instructs us "not to fear those who can kill the body, but cannot kill the soul; but rather to fear (revere) him who can destroy both soul and body in hell." We may well destroy each other, if not physically, then psychologically. We've seen plenty of each kind of destruction on both sides of every conflict, as we announce to the world, in the words of Bob Dylan, "God's on our side." Yet, we humans cannot destroy the spirit, the real self, try as we do.

The answer lies with our relationship to the living Lord of history. For Jesus' final words from the Cross were not, "My God, why have you forsaken me?" but, "Into your hands I commit my Spirit."

A woman complained bitterly about her pastor who ministered to her in a time of deep sorrow. "He had nothing new to tell me, just the same old business about Christ, the resurrection, nothing different, just the same old thing." What a contrast with a little boy sitting alone on the train. The pastor, noticing him, took a seat beside him and asked, "Aren't you afraid traveling alone like this?" "Oh, no," he replied. "My father is driving."

Of course, no matter how deeply committed to our faith, we will have bad days. Sometimes, in our agonizing, debilitating fears, we will cry out with Job, "Why was I born?" However, the Lord is in the driver's seat. God still controls the universe. Christ continues to care, more than we care for us, and for the world. He is Lord. We turn to him in our fears, because he first turned to us with his love.

Proper 8 • *Pentecost 6* • *Ordinary Time 13*

All Of This, And A Reward, Too?

Matthew 10:40-42

If we took this chapter seriously, we would probably wish that Matthew had never written it. Or, if he did write it, he should have eliminated the first 39 verses, and included only the last three. When we examine it carefully, or not so carefully, we discover that it turns our usual thinking about discipleship upside down.

I

Chapter 10 begins with God's call. God called the disciples from death to life. Some learned that accepting God's call would result in their early death. Yet, even if they had known in advance, still they would have responded. Following the call, God then commissions the disciples for their difficult task. "Don't even begin unless you're willing to persevere!" In verses 16-23, God continues to inform them of the dangers of their response. "See, I am sending you out like sheep into the midst of wolves; so be wise as serpents and innocent as doves." They would learn that truth only through the school of hard knocks. In verses 24-25, God probably startled them by encouraging them to be as Christ himself. And then, in verses 26-39, God consecrates them to their supreme task, to bear the Cross which could lead them to death, and in many instances did. No more doffing of one's hat to God, no mere using God for their purposes, no mere discipleship as convenience-store religion permitted. God called them to radical obedience.

We want to confine God's words, expectations, demands to a time long ago. We may think, would even like to think, that Jesus spoke specifically, and only specifically, to the twelve. Those non-sophisticates needed to get hit over the head to get the show on the road. Surely, this chapter applies only to them, not to us, now that we have "conquered the world for God." Don't you believe it! For unless we take the first part of this chapter seriously, we will never participate in the results. Chapter 10 begins with God's call to the original twelve and to us. It ends with a gift to them and to us.

II

Faith always begins with a gift, "The Incomparable," a title given to Seagram's distillery's top product some years ago. Faith always begins with God's grace, that unearned, undeserved, unmerited, unconditional acceptance of us as we are, here and now, not as we were yesterday, not as we will be tomorrow. Yet, most of us have great difficulty receiving anything, let alone the grace of God. The Scripture insists that "it's more blessed to give than receive"; but most of us have much more difficulty receiving than giving.

The twelve-year-old boy picked strawberries and beans one summer. As a surprise to his family, he spent hours choosing the right gifts for his parents and siblings. With pride and expectancy, he presented each gift. The only response came from his mother. "You shouldn't have done this."

Yes, how tough for us to receive. As a result, the New Year's card industry has bloomed in recent years. Why? Because we need a "legitimate" way to pay back those folks to whom we sent no cards, and whose cards to us arrived on December 26. We can't stand indebtedness to anyone, including God. We Protestants have created our own purgatory. A theology professor in a conservative Presbyterian seminary said to his class, "I doubt that more than five percent of us believe in the grace of God."

Once again, we abhor being in debt to God, so we seek to work our way, earn our way, climb our way into the Kingdom, by what we do and what we do not do. A Presbyterian elder, in his seventies, for the first time heard his pastor explain the meaning of grace. For years this elder performed every task in his local church to keep the institution perking. Then, when the pastor proclaimed that the Good News is free, the elder dejectedly responded, "I've been wasting my time all these years." Of course, he still failed to hear Good News. Yet, the Scripture says, over and over, entrance into the Kingdom is a gift. Either we receive the gift, or we do not. If we do not, God keeps pursuing us, until we say a final "No." The creed proclaims that "he descended into hell," still offering the gifts.

III

To those who receive and act upon the gift, Matthew, in the last three verses, focuses on the results of obedient suffering. Jesus affirms them for the dignity of their labors. He promises a reward for their faithful discipleship, extending to all who receive them.

The disciples, indeed, will suffer persecution, both from supposed friends inside and from obnoxious enemies outside the community. They learned, instantly, that, to take a stand, especially an unpopular one, invites criticism, often condemnation. Paul provides an additional clue in the Colossian letter. "I must fill up that which is lacking in the suffering of Christ." Have we ever heard Paul's statement? Paul speaks here, not about the natural suffering which comes to all of us; nor about playing Christian "kick-me" games; not about some physical toothache, or cancer, or AIDS, as crosses to endure (those are burdens, not crosses); nor about pathological, masochistic suffering as ends in themselves.

Paul speaks of suffering which results from, and only from, obedience to the Christ, no matter what the risks or consequences. Soren Kierkegaard points out that the decisive mark of the Christian is suffering, voluntary suffering. The compromising, acculturated church, the lukewarm church of Revelation has no idea what suffering for Christ means. Some of us are easily offended by any demand that we choose to suffer for any reason. Usually, we regard someone who makes a profound sacrifice for Christ's sake as lacking in common sense and good judgment. After all, we want no one to call us fanatics. Good grief, no! What humiliation! Yet, at the same time, our society encourages all kinds of fanaticism in sports, recreation, vocation, making-money schemes.

Take a simple, dreaded task with which most church sessions wrestle every year. "Whom shall we put on the inactive roll?" Not that one, his grandfather gave money for the organ fifty years ago. Not that one, she attended at Easter two years ago. Not that one, he gave $500 to the memorial fund (for his pet project). Not that one, she moved away fifteen years ago, and insists that we keep her name on the active roll. Most governing bodies take the easy way out to keep peace in the family, peace at all costs.

In the power of Christ, not all Christians back down and run away. In Ceylon, a high-caste person believes that God has called him to serve with the out-caste community. The high-caste members of his congregation have condemned his action, and have moved to a more congenial church. This man has been attacked in the streets, his house stoned. He has suffered severely for his commitment. As a result, he has become the most trusted friend of the out-caste community. His suffering has brought the members of that community into a knowledge of Jesus the Christ. This man has lived out the words of Karl Barth. "If there is no great agony in your heart, there will be no great words on your lips."

IV

Thank God, suffering never has the last word. Some will receive the disciples; some won't. That's God's business. Those who do receive the twelve, the extended twelve, namely, the church, receive Christ himself. Did we hear that promise? Those who receive them, and us, receive Christ! "Whoever gives to one of these little ones, that is, needy ones, even a cup of cold water, shall not lose his or her reward." Carl Jung's answer to Job, to us, drives home the truth. "To have nothing but God is everything."

David Livingstone lived what he believed. One day, he spoke at Glasgow University. As he rose to speak, he bore on his body the marks of his African struggles. Severe illnesses on nearly thirty occasions had left him gaunt and haggard. His left arm, crushed by a lion, hung helplessly at his side. After describing his trials and temptations, he asked, "Would you like me to tell you what supported me through all the years of exile among people whose language I could not understand and whose attitudes toward me were always uncertain and often hostile? It was this, 'Lo, I am with you always, even to the end of the world.' On those words, I staked everything, and they never failed."[1]

God calls us, sustains us along the way, and rewards us at the end. Christ always exhorts us to give our lives away, for the right reasons and causes, even when, especially when, we want to set the agenda, determine the route, to make it easy for us. God's Christ disturbs us when we take his mission seriously. God's Christ pushes us to change, to give up old, archaic, destructive behavior. God's Christ calls us out of our Egyptian slavery into the wilderness of our daily journey, into events in which we have no idea what the future holds.

Whatever our age, if we willingly lose our lives for Christ's sake and the good news, we will find our lives in obedience to the living Christ, in the Name of God the Creator, Liberator, Sustainer, Energizer. Amen.

---

1. From *Christian Century*. Source lost, date unknown.

Proper 9 • Pentecost 7 • Ordinary Time 14

It's Time!

Matthew 11:16-19, 25-30

"**Okay,** fellows. It's time. God has called you to your mission. God has commissioned you to your task. God has cautioned you about your status. God has encouraged you to be as I. God has consecrated you to your future. God has assured you of your reward. Now, get going! You will decide, by what you do now, if you are on my side, or not. Indeed, I am with you no matter what happens!" And, they went out, having little idea where the Christ would lead them.

I

Jesus offered no ordinary invitation. And they accepted the invitation only because he gave it. The biblical folks had waited ages for the Anointed One. They wanted to believe, yet it was a little too soon to put their whole being into that belief. John the Baptist, at Jesus' baptism, implies that Jesus is Messiah; but John still wavers. And the longer John languishes in prison, the more he wonders. "Are you he who is to come, or shall we look elsewhere?" No doubt, as the disciples travelled with Jesus, they would ask that same question a thousand times. How often have we asked that question to ourself, if not to another? In our pain, we cry out, "Where are you, Lord? Why won't you answer my prayers?"

Of course, we raise the wrong complaints, because, for some reason, we expect better treatment than that which Christ, himself, received. We often expect material rewards, power, prestige, popularity for our faithfulness. Our demands mimic those of the world around us. Even some clergy contribute to this expectation. "Send us your money, and you will be blessed. Support our ministry, and you will succeed." As a result, we have a tit-for-tat relationship with God. "You do this for me, Jesus; I'll do that for you." God abhors such games; and when we play them, we miss the essence of obedience and discipleship.

The Scripture clearly states that no one accepts the fact of Jesus' messiahship apart from repentance and acceptance of the Kingdom which the Messiah reveals. We cannot have one without the other. That Jesus is Messiah is an extraordinary fact that cannot be accepted without a change of heart, mind, and will. Our entrance into the Kingdom first begins with an act of God. God offers us grace, that is, unconditional acceptance, as a gift. Our life in Christ begins, not when I say, "I gave my life to Jesus," but when I acknowledge God's free gift to me. To reverse the process puts us back into the Protestant purgatory. "What must I do?" What we do is to receive the gift.

To repent, however, literally means to change our way of thinking and doing. The French word, *repensir*, means to rethink. The Greek word means to reverse our field. We've been running one direction, our direction; and now, we change directions. Only the Spirit of the Messiah makes that change possible. If left to our own devices, we will accept Frank Sinatra's theme song, "I do it my way." If left to ourselves, we will live out Sigmund Freud's Pleasure Principle, "I want what I want when I want it; and never mind the consequences." The Bible calls such behavior living in sin, living the I-centered life. Sadly, we have softened the word "sin," and thus, have diminished the need for repentance.

The softening process is subtle and seductive, especially in the institutional church. We see, on some church buildings, "Christ is the answer." Really? What's the question? Or, we hear, even use, the phrase, "The family that prays together stays together." Really? Why do we have divorces among faithful church members, as several new members of the Republican Congress discovered in 1995? Or, come and hear our pastor preach, our choir sing; enjoy our fellowship. They don't like the sermon. The choir sings off key. No one speaks to them. Carlyle Marney, in his book *Structures of Prejudice*, insists that the "church's point of contact with the world must be a point of conflict with the world. That point of contact is sin." Our approach is to talk about everything but repentance, hoping that the pastor will deal with the subject in the prospective member class. Not likely. Unfortunately, we give the impression that the Messiah has come to solve our problems, as *we* see those problems. If so presented, the Messiah, then, is not one who defines our salvation, but simply provides the salvation that we define, and for which we long. In effect, then, we humans offer a new life without death to the old ways, resurrection without crucifixion, Easter without Good Friday. The gospel makes no such offer. Repentance is required for entrance into the Messiah's Kingdom. And, if we are not offended by the claim of God's Kingdom upon us, we are indeed blessed, fulfilled.

II

Again, only the Presence and Power of the Christ reveal that life-changing truth to us. No amount of positive or possibility thinking will make it happen. In no way do we achieve, attain, the knowledge of God by our own devices. It comes only and always as God's gift to us through Holy Spirit. Only the Son reveals the Father. Therefore, it is not the world's wise ones, wise guys and gals, who know God. It is those who have seen God in the work and ministry of the Son. And those who see God at work in Jesus, those whom Jesus chooses to reveal God, are not the wise or self-righteous, but the repentant, the lowly, the world's "nobodies," those who recognize their real need, namely, a true relationship with the living God.

For the repenters, Jesus now comes with hope for our living as responsibly free and freely responsible persons, rather than merely existing as slaves to the details and distractions of human laws. "Come to me, all of you who are exhausted and weighed down beneath your burdens, self-imposed or other-imposed, and I will give you rest (zest) ... My yoke is easy; my burden is light" (author's translation).

Jesus speaks here to people desperately trying to find God, as if God were lost; desperately trying to enter the Kingdom by obedience to human laws; and thus, driven to weariness and despair.

"Come to me, my yoke is easy." The Greek word means "well-fitting," that is, "tailor made to fit the ox." A legend tells that Jesus made the best ox-yoke in all of Galilee. People from everywhere came to his dad's carpenter shop to buy them. In those days, as today, shops had their signs above the door. Some suggested that the sign above the door in Jesus' shop read, "My yoke fits well."

Jesus is telling us this about yokes and burdens: "The life I give you is meant, not as a burden to gall you; but as a measure to fit you, my burden is light. If you try to do it all yourself, you'll come to the end puzzled, angry, exhausted, unfulfilled." A four-year-old kindergartner caught the essence of Jesus' truth, "My yoke is easy...." Turning to the children, the teacher asked, "Who can tell me what a yoke is?" The little girl replied, "Something they put on the necks of animals, as we have on our models in the barnyard." "What's the meaning of God's yoke?" inquired the teacher. All were quiet, and then the hand of the four-year-old shot up. "That's when God puts His arms around our neck."[1]

Nowhere does God promise that the burden is easy to carry. God does lay it on us in love, knowing what's better for us than we know for ourselves. God does invite us to carry it in love, for love makes the heaviest burden light. Boys' Town of Nebraska has adopted this story as its theme: A man came upon a little boy carrying on his back a still smaller boy who was lame. "That's a heavy burden for you to carry," said the man. The boy replied, "He's no burden for me; he's my brother."

---

1. A. P. Bailey, *Indianapolis Star*.

Proper 10 • Pentecost 8 • Ordinary Time 15

4000 Chickens And 2000 Eggs

Matthew 13:1-9, 18-23

One autumn, a young man aiming for the seminary left home to complete his college degree. When he returned in the spring, his parents had gone into the chicken-for-eggs business. To that point, he knew little about chickens, except for the fact that they made an excellent dinner. He learned quickly, however, that to call a person a chicken, though perhaps appropriate, is not an act of admiration. For the novice, nothing is more nauseating than a chicken house full of chickens. He decided, nevertheless, to learn about chickens. His dad enlightened him that every chicken house contains four kinds of chickens. When he heard the descriptions, he thought of Jesus' parable about the seeds and the soils. So today, I offer to you this message about chickens and soils and people.

I

"Listen! A sower went out to sow. And as he sowed, some seeds fell on the path, and the birds came and ate them up." Jesus interprets this soil. "When anyone hears the word of the kingdom and does not understand it, the evil one comes and snatches away what is sown in the heart; this is what was sown on the path." When the sower scattered the seeds, they fell on hardpan soil, with no opportunity for the seed to get established, and thus, no opportunity to grow.

Caution: please refrain from pushing the analysis too far. We will see both similarities and dissimilarities between seeds, chickens, and people.

The first seed and soil reminded me of the first group of chickens, the "pullets." Pullets are young, immature birds, too young to produce. They are in the process of preparing for later life, when they will begin to lay eggs. The desire of the pullet, if pullets have desire, is to become a productive member of the hen house.

The church, we hope, has many pullets, boys and girls too young to produce in the same way as adults. Yet, please never refer to children as "the church of the future." They are the church of "now." And, they need our nurturing to help them develop their potential. We adult members make that promise to them in *our* membership vows and *their* baptismal vows.

So, with the seed which fell on the path, the potential for growth is present, but can be fulfilled only if it sinks roots into the ground. With the pullet, the potential also is present. The pullet's potential will be realized only after painstaking care by the farmer. All kinds of things can happen, and happen quickly, to destroy a whole flock of chickens — disease, crowding together, fire. With children, the potential is present. However, only with a parent or parent-substitute will those children become fully human, fully productive, a complete member of society, an integral member of the community of faith. That is our privilege and responsibility.

II

"Other seeds fell on rocky ground, where they did not have much soil, and they sprang up quickly, since they had no depth of soil. But when the sun rose, they were scorched; and since they had no root, they withered away." Jesus explains: "As for what was sown on rocky ground, this is the one who hears the word and immediately receives it with joy; yet such a person has no root, but endures only for a while, and when trouble or persecution arises on account of the word, that person immediately falls away." Some hear the word, and receive it with joy. With no root, they endure only a short time. When they're put to the test, they fall away. Yes, this person does have potential for growth. These folks began as roman candles in the church. Many of these joined the church after John Kennedy's death. And soon dropped out.

The second chicken, the molter, goes temporarily or permanently out of production. Now, this is a natural and necessary process; but some molt frequently; so the farmer cuts them from the flock. In the church, this becomes the annual trimming-the-roll exercise.

These church members give their all for Jesus and the church for a few months or years. Then, they disappear. A man joined the church one Sunday. Immediately, he asked what he could do. No one turns down a volunteer. He ushered, he cleaned up the sanctuary after worship. He became a deacon. When others asked if they could assist him, he always said, "No. I'll do it." For five years, he did it all, and he did it "my way." Then, he began to complain and gripe because he "had to do it all, and no one would help me." A few weeks later, he left the church. When the honeymoon is over, some members go out of production. We all need temporary rests; but for many, this "temporary" becomes permanent. So, if we have moved from the pullet stage, have we decided to rest temporarily or permanently in the molting stage?

III

"Other seeds fell among thorns, and the thorns grew up and choked them." Jesus clarifies. "As for what was sown among thorns, this is the one who hears the word, but the cares of the world and the lure of wealth choke the word, and it yields nothing." Again, the seeds have begun to realize their potential. They remind us of some fields, mustard fields which are supposed to be clover fields. In only a short time, the mustard takes over the whole field; the other plants suffocate and die.

This third seed/soil identifies the third group, the cluckers. The cluckers, too, go out of production temporarily. They waltz around the chicken house pretending that they are productive; but their only productivity is clucking. The cluckers are noisy, loud, and great-pretenders. A second quality of the clucker is that it insists on incubating the eggs which it has not laid.

In the church's life, the cluckers become the complainers, criticizers, condemners. These folks spend considerable time and energy clucking about what they don't like. They never quite get around to cluck about what is right, good, and positive. These dart-flingers have a never-ending supply of ammunition. These people contribute to the destruction of marriages, even those they attend. They ignore the pastor's invitation. "If anyone knows any legitimate reason why these two should not be married, speak now, or from now on, keep your mouth shut." Unfortunately, most cluckers keep on clucking, and hear nothing but the sound of their clucking. Chicken cluckers are culled from the flock. Church cluckers may remain in a congregation until the day they die. Ultimately, Jesus will cull them from the flock. "I never knew you."

IV

And then, once more: "Other seeds fell on good soil and brought forth grain, some a hundredfold, some sixty, some thirty. Let anyone with ears listen!" Jesus clarifies: "But as for what was sown on good soil, this is the one who hears the word and understands it, who indeed bears fruit and yields, in one case a hundred fold, in another sixty, and in another thirty." These are the pride and joy of the sower. These make the planting worthwhile. This fourth group, the layers, also is the pride and joy of the farmer. These mature birds produce daily. They bear the burden for the rest of the flock. The layers make up for all of the non-producers, the pullets, molters, cluckers.

In the institutional church, these people realize that they must lose their life to find it, must share their life to save it, must give their life to have it. Some of them tithe their time, talents, treasure. Some are pray-ers, who keep an open circuit between God, self, others. They are not crisis-oriented Christians. Some are teachers, choir members, church officers, and active participants. They recognize that they, not the pastor, are the ministers, priests, saints in communion.

So, which soil, which chicken, which person do you represent? I invite us to suppose for a few minutes. Suppose that the membership of this church were limited to 100 people. Would you be in or out? Suppose that you had to "run" for church membership. Would you win or lose? Suppose that membership were good for one year only, and that reelection depended upon what you had done in the church's life during that time. Would you be reelected? Suppose that there were a long waiting list of those desiring to get in. Would your name appear on the list? Suppose that you were called on to tell why you thought that the church should keep your name on the roll. Have you a record of helpful services to offer in self-defense? Suppose that every member of the church did just as much as you're doing right now. Would more room be needed, or would the doors be shut and nailed?[1]

Some seeds fell on good soil and brought forth grain, some a hundredfold, some sixty, some thirty. Those who have ears to hear, listen, and listen carefully, for God's sake, for the world's sake, for your sake. Amen!

---

1. From a denominational newsletter, source lost.

Proper 11 • *Pentecost 9* • *Ordinary Time 16*

The Eternal Divorce

Matthew 13:24-30, 36-43

What's your first image when you hear these parables describing the kingdom of God in Matthew 13? Remember that the kingdom of God defines the reign of God; that is, wherever God reigns, there is the kingdom. Our danger, of course, is to know what the parables say before reading them, either because the stories are too familiar; or, we quote bits and pieces out of context; or, we forget that they represent only a part of the good news.

Unlike some of us, Jesus was no cynic. Not once during his misunderstood, misjudged life did he throw up his hands, and cry out, "What's the use? I can do nothing for the highest creation. They insist on going to hell; so let them go. Everyone's going to the dogs. Let them go!" No, Jesus, despite his horrible death, refused to look at, relate to, the world through pessimistic eyes.

Jesus, also, was no blind, giddy, utopian optimist either. No biblical author records anywhere that Jesus saw an easy way out of the human condition. No one put these shallow words into Jesus' mouth: "People and events are getting better and better. With a little more education, enlightenment, people will create their own heaven." No indeed, Jesus never looked at us humans through rose-colored glasses.

Indeed, this carpenter-savior knew precisely what is in us. His look could penetrate every social smile to unmask the real person. And because of his insight and awareness, he could bring together a healthy relationship between pessimism, which leads to despair, and optimism, which leads to illusion. In the parable of the wheat and the weeds, he shows us how.

I

Jesus begins the story on a vigorous note. "The kingdom of heaven is like a person who sowed good seed in his field." Jesus wasted no words. Then, just as quickly, as with many of Jesus' parables, it took a sudden reverse turn. He offers no explanation as to why. "While the farm hands were sleeping, the farmer's enemy came and sowed weeds among the wheat." What a rotten trick, even more rotten than it appears on the surface. The midnight gardener picked a weed which the farmer could not distinguish immediately from the wheat. Not until the wheat blossomed did the farmer discover that his enemy had sprinkled the field with the subtle weed. What should he do? The farm hands insisted, "Pull the weeds out! Now!" However, while pulling out the darnel, they would also pull out much of the wheat. So, the farmer, in his wisdom, decided to let them grow together.

Now, even though we find the parable interesting, what exactly did Jesus want the disciples and us to know? Simply this. The good and evil live and grow together, within the same community, same world. For God makes the sun rise on the evil and good, and sends rain on the just and unjust. God provides both the same atmosphere; breathing the same air, polluted or pure; feeling warmth from the same sun; sharing the same bus; residing in the same neighborhood. The just and unjust live side by side, sometimes under the same roof. The farmer refused to succumb to the demands of the hired hands. "Let's pull out the weeds!" Those farm hands had no zeal for tolerating the mixture, no desire for coexistence.

Isn't this our usual approach? Isn't this how we prefer to handle the difficult situation, the intolerable person? Years ago, when only the United States owned the atomic bomb, some people, inside and outside of the church, urged our leaders, "Blast the Soviets while we still have the chance!" We disagree with the teacher or pastor; so, either we try to remove the person, or if we can't do that, we remove ourselves and our children. We make certain assumptions about certain people, so we eliminate them from our communities by establishing laws which keep them out.

II

We see that neither the farmer nor Jesus handled matters that way at all. Let them grow together. Of course, it's dangerous. Maybe evil, at least temporarily, maybe for centuries, will overpower the truth. The opposite also may work. The good may have, often does have, a powerful life-changing influence on the evil. We see that happen among husbands and wives, between parents and children. We have learned the absolute necessity of coexistence or no-existence.

Again, we may experience this truth in our home. A husband and wife may find themselves at opposite poles intellectually or spiritually. (How did they ever get together in the first place? If we've ever been married, we know.) How will they deal with their crisis? Pull out? Run away? Get divorced? Not if this parable means what it says, corroborated in 1 Corinthians 7. "A man who has a non-Christian wife who is willing to live with him should not divorce her. A wife, in a similar position, should not divorce her husband. For the unbelieving husband is in a sense 'consecrated' by being joined to his wife; the unbelieving wife is similarly 'consecrated' by the Christian husband she has married ... And, after all, how can you, who are a wife, know whether you will be able to save your husband or not? And the same applies to you who are a husband." "Let them grow together," insist Jesus and Paul. We have no idea how one will influence the other. Obviously, this is dangerous living. The good may give in to the evil. Evil attitudes and influences may swamp the good, at least temporarily, often permanently.

Jesus takes this risk with us when he permits the good and evil to live side-by-side. Because of our mixed-existence, Jesus' keynote address to us highlights the words "patience" and "perseverance." These words fall on deaf ears to many Americans, many Christians. "Patience, perseverance accomplish nothing. Waiting takes too much time. I want what I want now!" Think of young marrieds, with or without parental help, who buy, through credit cards, everything the first year of their marriage, which took their parents fifteen or twenty years to accumulate. And so, as lemmings rushing headlong into the sea, we rush headlong into financial, then emotional, then spiritual oblivion. Nels Ferré correctly warns, "The less we are willing to wait, the less we believe in God." "Root out the evil now, at least the evil in others," we insist. "Patience, perseverance, let the two grow together," Jesus insists. Certainly, Jesus hates evil. He wants it rooted out more than we, not through foolhardy impatience, but through loving patience.

III

The parable does end on a note of judgment. The farmer, at harvest time, must separate the wheat for the hayloft, and toss the darnel into the fire. The farmer knew, if he wanted to harvest a usable crop, he would need to wait until threshing time.

According to the parable, we are no different. As tasteless as the final judgment is to us, still, we will face it as victors or victims. On the last day, or our last day, Christ will separate the evil, or perhaps, the evil will separate itself, from all of society, from all godly influences, not necessarily to a fiery furnace, but to a state or place from which all influences of God exist. The righteous, that is, the ones who have accepted the righteousness of God for their lives, take up eternal residence in God's kingdom. The unrighteous, those who say "No" to God, are delivered to eternal punishment or separation. Sounds cruel, doesn't it, especially with a loving God, to think that some live forever apart from God, while others "enjoy God forever." When we grasp the significance of life, of eternity with or apart from God, we begin to understand the terror and horror of hell, apart from all that is holy, just, pure. "It's not fair!" some plead. "No loving God would ever do this to anyone, no matter how evil; surely, we must have a second chance after we die," others hope. No wonder that many of us, for all practical purposes, believe in no hell, or only hell on earth, or hell only for those whom we hate and despise.

We can blame God all we want. We can insist that life isn't fair. The fact remains, however, that we choose. Each day, we decide to live as God's person or our own. We judge ourselves by our lives, by the fruits of our decisions. Still, we may protest, "If people really had an honest chance to see and explore the kingdom, they would choose nothing less than the kingdom." Really? Do we not often choose exactly the opposite of what will do us, and those around us, the most good? We know precisely what we need to do for healthy relationships, and then, turn around and act as though we never hear our inner voice. We know the results of our destructive actions; yet we go right on doing those behaviors that get us into trouble anyway. If we have ever had an extramarital affair, study the process. Where did we get the idea that the beginning of eternity transforms our entire personality from evil to good in a flash? It seems logical to believe that evil people continue their evil pursuits, while good persons, more than ever, choose to please God.

Still, some insist, "I have a neighbor (or relative) who does not believe in the Christ. He's such a good man. Surely, God wouldn't have the heart to keep him out of the kingdom." Check out your assumptions. Ask that person if he wants to spend eternity with God. If he says, "Yes," ask him how much time he spends with God now. If he spends little or no time with God now, why should he want to spend eternity with God? God gives us the freedom to decide to be in hell, to go to hell. That's how much God loves us.

According to this parable, final separation occurs. Divorce is an ugly sight, any way we look at it. Eternal divorce from God horrifies the sensitive, and not so sensitive, mind. Perhaps some of us have no great concern about our, or another's, eternal destiny. Perhaps we believe that God will welcome all of us into the pearly gates. We can play games around God and eternity all we want, pretending we are in when we are not. Now however, during the light, now is the hour to decide. Jesus gives us plenty of warning. "The way is narrow that leads to eternal life, and few there are who shall find it."

The wheat and weeds grow together. The day comes, sooner than we want or expect, when they, and we, are separated and treated differently. "And that's the truth," as Lily Tomlin insists.

Lectionary Preaching After Pentecost

Virtually all pastors who make use of the sermons in this book will find their worship life and planning shaped by one of two lectionary series. Most mainline Protestant denominations, along with clergy of the Roman Catholic Church, have now approved — either for provisional or official use — the three-year Revised Common (Consensus) Lectionary. This family of denominations includes United Methodist, Presbyterian, United Church of Christ and Disciples of Christ. Recently the ELCA division of Lutheranism also began following the Revised Common Lectionary. This change has been reflected in the headings and scripture listings with each sermon in this book.

Roman Catholics and Lutheran divisions other than ELCA follow their own three-year cycle of texts. While there are divergences between the Revised Common and Roman Catholic/Lutheran systems, the gospel texts show striking parallels, with few text selections evidencing significant differences. Nearly all the gospel texts included in this book will, therefore, be applicable to worship and preaching planning for clergy following either lectionary.

A significant divergence does occur, however, in the method by which specific gospel texts are assigned to specific calendar days. The Revised Common and Roman Catholic Lectionaries accomplish this by counting backwards from Christ the King (Last Sunday after Pentecost), discarding "extra" texts from the front of the list: Lutherans (not using the Revised Common Lectionary) follow the opposite pattern, counting forward from The Holy Trinity, discarding "extra" texts at the end of the list.

The following index will aid the user of this book in matching the correct text to the correct Sunday during the Pentecost portion of the church year.

(Fixed dates do not pertain to Lutheran Lectionary)

Fixed Date Lectionaries	**Lutheran Lectionary**
Revised Common (including ELCA) and Roman Catholic	*Lutheran*
The Day of Pentecost	The Day of Pentecost
The Holy Trinity	The Holy Trinity
May 29-June 4 — Proper 4, Ordinary Time 9	Pentecost 2
June 5-11 — Proper 5, Ordinary Time 10	Pentecost 3
June 12-18 — Proper 6, Ordinary Time 11	Pentecost 4
June 19-25 — Proper 7, Ordinary Time 12	Pentecost 5

June 26-July 2 — Proper 8, Ordinary Time 13	Pentecost 6
July 3-9 — Proper 9, Ordinary Time 14	Pentecost 7
July 10-16 — Proper 10, Ordinary Time 15	Pentecost 8
July 17-23 — Proper 11, Ordinary Time 16	Pentecost 9
July 24-30 — Proper 12, Ordinary Time 17	Pentecost 10
July 31-Aug. 6 — Proper 13, Ordinary Time 18	Pentecost 11
Aug. 7-13 — Proper 14, Ordinary Time 19	Pentecost 12
Aug. 14-20 — Proper 15, Ordinary Time 20	Pentecost 13
Aug. 21-27 — Proper 16, Ordinary Time 21	Pentecost 14
Aug. 28-Sept. 3 — Proper 17, Ordinary Time 22	Pentecost 15
Sept. 4-10 — Proper 18, Ordinary Time 23	Pentecost 16
Sept. 11-17 — Proper 19, Ordinary Time 24	Pentecost 17
Sept. 18-24 — Proper 20, Ordinary Time 25	Pentecost 18
Sept. 25-Oct. 1 — Proper 21, Ordinary Time 26	Pentecost 19
Oct. 2-8 — Proper 22, Ordinary Time 27	Pentecost 20
Oct. 9-15 — Proper 23, Ordinary Time 28	Pentecost 21
Oct. 16-22 — Proper 24, Ordinary Time 29	Pentecost 22
Oct. 23-29 — Proper 25, Ordinary Time 30	Pentecost 23
Oct. 30-Nov. 5 — Proper 26, Ordinary Time 31	Pentecost 24
Nov. 6-12 — Proper 27, Ordinary Time 32	Pentecost 25
Nov. 13-19 — Proper 28, Ordinary Time 33	Pentecost 26
	Pentecost 27
Nov. 20-26 — Christ the King	Christ the King

Reformation Day (or last Sunday in October) is October 31 (Revised Common, Lutheran)

All Saints' Day (or first Sunday in November) is November 1 (Revised Common, Lutheran, Roman Catholic)

Books In This Cycle A Series

GOSPEL SET

And Then Came The Angel
Sermons for Advent/Christmas/Epiphany
William B. Kincaid, III

The Lord Is Risen! He Is Risen Indeed! He Really Is!
Sermons For Lent/Easter
Richard L. Sheffield

No Post-Easter Slump
Sermons For Sundays After Pentecost (First Third)
Wayne H. Keller

We Walk By Faith
Sermons For Sundays After Pentecost (Middle Third)
Richard Gribble

Where Gratitude Abounds
Sermons For Sundays After Pentecost (Last Third)
Joseph M. Freeman

FIRST LESSON SET

Between Gloom And Glory
Sermons For Advent/Christmas/Epiphany
R. Glen Miles

Cross, Resurrection, And Ascension
Sermons For Lent/Easter
Richard Gribble

Is Anything Too Wonderful For The Lord?
Sermons For Sundays After Pentecost (First Third)
Leonard W. Mann

The Divine Salvage
Sermons For Sundays After Pentecost (Middle Third)
R. Curtis and Tempe Fussell

When God Says, "Let Me Alone"
Sermons For Sundays After Pentecost (Last Third)
William A. Jones

SECOND LESSON SET

Moving At The Speed Of Light
Sermons For Advent/Christmas/Epiphany
Frank Luchsinger

Love Is Your Disguise
Sermons For Lent/Easter
Frank Luchsinger

www.ingramcontent.com/pod-product-compliance
Lightning Source LLC
Chambersburg PA
CBHW071759040426
42446CB00012B/2622